IMPURE
LUST

GW00706149

IMPURE
LUST

John Flavel

From Flavel's *The Harlot's Face
in the Scripture-Glass*

THE BANNER OF TRUTH TRUST

THE BANNER OF TRUTH TRUST
3 Murrayfield Road, Edinburgh EH12 6EL, UK
P.O. Box 621, Carlisle, PA 17013, USA

*

© Banner of Truth Trust 2008

ISBN-13: 978 0 85151 981 4

*

Typeset in 10.5 / 13.5 pt Adobe Caslon Pro
at the Banner of Truth Trust, Edinburgh

Printed in the USA by
Versa Press, Inc.,
East Peoria, IL

IMPURE LUST

*T*he danger I shall give you warning of is the sin of uncleanness; with which I fear too many of the rude and looser sort of seamen defile themselves; and possibly, the temptations to this sin are advantaged and strengthened upon them more than others by their condition and employments. Let no man be offended that I here give warning of this evil: I intend to asperse no man's person, or raise up jealousy against any; but would faithfully discharge my duty to all, and that in all things. It was the complaint of Salvian many hundred years ago, that he could not speak against the vices of men, but one or other would thus object, 'There he meant me; he hit me': and so storm and fret. Alas (as he replied) it is not 'we that speak to you, but your own conscience; we speak to the order, but conscience speaks to the person.' I shall use no other apology in this case.

That this sin is a dreadful gulf, a quick-sand that has sucked in and destroyed thousands, is truly apparent both from Scripture and experience. Solomon tells us, *Prov.* 22:14, that it is a 'deep ditch, into which such as are abhorred of the LORD shall fall'. Oh! the multitudes of dead that are there! and if so, I cannot in duty to God, or in love to you, be silent, where the danger is so great.

It is both needless, and beside my intention here to insist largely upon the explication of the particulars in which uncleanness is distributed; the more ordinary and common sins of this kind are known by the names of adultery and fornication. The latter is when single persons come together out of the state of marriage. The former is when at least one of the persons committing uncleanness is contracted in marriage. This now is the evil I shall warn you of. And, that you may never fall into this pit, I shall endeavour to hedge and fence up the way to it by these ensuing arguments: and, oh! that the light of every argument may be powerfully reflected upon your conscience!

Many men are wise in generals, but very vain in the reasonings or imaginations, as the apostle calls them, *Rom.* 1:21. that is, in their *practical inferences.* They are good at speculation, but bunglers at application: but it is truth in the particulars that, like a hot iron, pierces; and, oh! that you may find these to be such in your soul! To that end consider,

ARGUMENT 1

The names and titles by which this sin is known in Scripture are very vile and base.

The Spirit of God, doubtless, has put such odious names upon it on purpose to deter and frighten men from it. In general it is called *lust;* and so (as one notes) it bears the name of its mother; it is *uncleanness* in the abstract, *Num.* 5:19, *filthiness* itself; *an abomination, Ezek.* 22:11. And they that commit it are called *abominable, Rev.* 21:8. Varro says the word imports that which is not lawful to mention; or rather, abominable persons, such as are not fit for the society of men, such as should be hissed out of all men's company: they are rather to be reckoned beasts than men. Yea, the Scripture compares them to the filthiest of beasts, even to dogs. When Ishbosheth charged this sin upon Abner, 2 *Sam.* 3:8, he said, 'Am I a dog's head that thou chargest me with a fault concerning this woman?' And in *Deut.* 23:18 the hire of a whore, and 'the price of a dog', are put together. The expression of this lust in words or gesture, is called *neighing, Jer.* 5:8. Even as fed horses do, that scatter their lust promiscuously. Or, if the Scripture speaks of them as men, yet it allows them but the external shape of men, not the understanding of men. Among the Jews they were called fools in Israel, 2 *Sam.* 13:13, and so *Prov.* 6:32. 'Whoso committeth adultery with a woman, lacketh understanding'. And sinners, *Luke* 7:37: 'And, behold, a woman which was a sinner', that is, an eminent notorious sinner: by which term the Scripture deciphers an unclean person, as if, among sinners, there were none of such a prodigious stature in sin as they.

And we find that when the Spirit of God would set forth any sin by an odious name, he calls it adultery; so idolatry is called adultery, *Ezek.* 16:32.

And indeed this spiritual and corporeal adultery oftentimes are found in the same persons. They that give themselves up to the one are, by the righteous hand of God given up to the other, as it is too manifestly and frequently exemplified in the world. So earthly-mindedness has this name put upon it on purpose to frighten men from it, *James* 4:4. Now certainly God would never borrow the name of this sin to set out the evil of other sins if it were not most vile and abominable. It is called the sin of the Gentiles, or heathens, 1 *Thess.* 4:5. And, oh that we could say, it were only among them that know not God!

How then are you able to look these Scriptures in the face, and not blush? O what a sin is this! Are you willing to be ranked with fools, dogs, sinners, heathens, and take your lot with them? God has planted that affection of shame in your nature to be as a guard against such filthy lusts; it is a sin that has filthiness enough in it to defile the tongue that mentions it, *Eph.* 5:3.

Argument 2

It is a sin that the God of heaven has often prohibited and severely condemned in the Word, which abundantly declares his abhorrence of it.

You have prohibition upon prohibition, and threatening upon threatening in the word against it; *Exod.* 20:14. 'Thou shalt not commit adultery.' This was delivered upon mount Sinai with the greatest solemnity and terror by the mouth of God himself. Turn to, and ponder the following Scriptures among many others, *Prov.* 5:2–4; *Acts* 5:29; *Rom.* 1:24, 29; 13:13; 1 *Cor.* 6:13–18; 2 *Cor.*

12:21. *Gal.* 5:29; *Eph.* 5:3. *Col.* 3:5. 1 *Thess.* 4:2–5. *Heb.* 12:16; 13:4. All these, with many others, are the true sayings of God: by them you shall be tried in the last day.

Now, consider how terrible it will be to have so many words of God, and such terrible ones too as most of those are, to be brought in and pleaded against your soul in that day! Mountains and hills may depart, but these words shall not depart: heaven and earth shall pass away, but not one tittle of the word shall pass away.

Believe it, sinner, as sure as the heavens are over your head, and the earth under your feet, they shall one day take hold of you, though we poor worms who plead them with you, die and perish: *Zech.* 1:5–6. The Lord tells us it shall not fall to the ground – which is a borrowed speech from a dart that is flung with a weak hand; it goes not home to the mark, but falls to the ground by the way. None of these words shall so fall to the ground.

ARGUMENT 3

It is a sin that defiles and destroys the body; 1 Cor. 6:18. *'He that committeth adultery, sinneth against his own body.'*

In most other sins the body is the *instrument*, here it is the *object* against which the sin is committed: that body of yours, which should be the temple of the Holy Spirit, is turned into a sty of filthiness; yea, it not only defiles, but destroys it. Job calls it a 'fire that burneth to destruction', *Job* 31:12. or as the Septuagint reads it, a fire that burns in all the members. It is a sin that God has plagued with strange and terrible diseases, *Rom.* 1:30. These were judgments sent immediately by God's own hand, to correct the new sins and enormities of the world.

Oh how terrible is it to lie groaning under the sad effects of this sin! As Solomon tells us, *Prov.* 5:11: 'And thou mourn at the last, when thy flesh and thy body are consumed.' To this sense some expound that terrible text, *Heb.* 13:4 'Marriage is honourable in all, and the bed undefiled; but whoremongers and adulterers God will judge'; i.e. with some remarkable judgment inflicted on them in this world: if it escape the punishment of men, it shall not escape the vengeance of God. Ah, with what comfort may a man lie down upon a sick-bed, when the sickness can be looked upon as a fatherly visitation coming in mercy! But you that shorten your life, and bring sickness on yourself by such a sin are the devil's martyr; and to whom can you turn in such a day for comfort?

ARGUMENT 4

Consider what an indelible blot it is to your nature, which can never be wiped away; though you escape with your life, yet, as one says, you shall be burnt in the hand, yea, branded in the forehead.

What a foul scar is that upon the face of David himself, which abides to this day: 'He was upright in all things, save in the matter of Uriah.' And how was he slighted by his own children and servants after he had committed this sin! Compare 1 *Sam.*

2:30. with 2 *Sam.* 11:10–11. 'A wound and dishonour shall he get': and his reproach shall not be wiped away.' This is to give your 'honour to another', *Prov.* 5:9. The shame and reproach attending it should be a preservative from it. Indeed the devil tempts to it by hopes of secrecy and concealment; but though many other sins lie hid, and possibly shall never come to light until that day of manifestation of all hidden things, yet this is a sin that is most usually discovered.

Under the law, God appointed an extraordinary way for the discovery of it, *Num.* 5:13. And to this day the providence of God does often very strangely bring it to light, though it be a deed of darkness: the Lord has many times brought such persons, either by terror of conscience, frenzy, or some other means, to be the publishers and proclaimers of their own shame. Yea, observe this, said the reverend Mr Hildersham [Arthur Hildersham, 1563–1632] on John chapter 4, even those that are most cunning to conceal and hide it from the eye of the world, yet through the just judgment of God, everyone suspects and condemns them for it: this dashes in pieces, at one stroke, that vessel in which the precious ointment of a good name is carried. A fool in Israel shall be your title; and even children shall point at you.

ARGUMENT 5

*It scatters your substance, and roots
up the foundation of your estate;*
Job 31:12: *It roots up all increase.*

Strangers 'shall be filled with thy wealth,
and thy labours shall be in the house of
a stranger', *Prov.* 5:10. 'For by means of
a whorish woman, a man is brought to a
morsel of bread', *Prov.* 6:26. It gives rags
for its livery (says one) and though it be
furthered by fulness, yet it is *followed* with a
morsel of bread.

This is one of those temporal judgments
with which God punishes the unclean
person in this life. The word Delilah, which
is the name of a harlot, is conceived to come
from a root that signifies to exhaust, drain,
or draw dry. This sin will quickly exhaust

the fullest estate; and, oh! what a dreadful thing will this be, when God shall require an account of your stewardship in the great day! How righteous it is that that man should be fuel to the wrath of God, whose health and wealth have been so much fuel to maintain the flame of lust! O how lavish of their estates are sinners to satisfy their lusts! If the members of Christ be sick or in prison, they may there perish and starve before they will relieve them; but to obtain their lusts, Oh, how expensive! 'Ask me never so much, and I will give it'; says Shechem! *Gen.* 34:19 'Ask what thou wilt, and it shall be given thee', said Herod to the daughter of Herodias. Well, you are liberal in spending treasures upon your lusts; and believe it, God will spend treasures of wrath to punish you for your lusts.

It had been a thousand times better for you if you had never had an estate, that you had begged your bread from door to door, than to have such a sad reckoning as you shall shortly have for it.

ARGUMENT 6

Oh, stand off from this sin, because it is a pit out of which very few have been recovered that have fallen therein.

Few are the footsteps of returners from this den. The longer a man lives in it, the less power he has to leave it. It is not only a *damning*, but an *infatuating* sin. The danger of falling this way must needs be great, and the fall very desperate; because few that fall into it do ever rise again.

Flavel on Lust 21

I shall lay two very terrible Scriptures before you to this purpose, either of them enough to drive you speedily to Christ, or to drive you out of your wits; one is Ecclesiastes 7:26. 'And I find more bitter than death, the woman whose heart is snares and nets, and her hands as bands: Whoso pleaseth God shall escape from her, but the sinner shall be taken by her.' The argument which the Spirit of God uses here to dissuade from this sin is taken from the *subject;* they that fall into it, for the most part, are persons in whom God has no delight, and so in judgment are delivered up to it, and never recovered by grace from it.

The other text is Proverbs 22:14. 'The mouth of a strange woman is a deep pit; he that is abhorred of the LORD shall fall therein.' O terrible word! Able to daunt the heart of the securest sinner. Your whores *embrace* you, yea, but God *abhors* you! You have their *love*, oh but you are under God's *hatred!*

What say you to these two Scriptures? If you are not atheists, I think such a word from the mouth of God should strike like a dart through your soul. And upon this account it is that they never are recovered, because God has no delight in them.

If this be not enough, view one Scripture more, Proverbs 2:18–19. 'For her house inclineth unto death, and her paths unto the dead: None that go to her, return again, neither take they hold of the paths of life.' Reader, if you be a person addicted to this sin, go your way, and think seriously what a case you are in. *None return again*, i.e. a very few of many: the examples of such as have been recovered are very rare.

Pliny tells us, the mermaids are commonly seen in green meadows, and have enchanting voices; but there are always found heaps of dead men's bones lying by them. This may be but a fabulous story: but I am sure it is true of the harlot, whose siren songs have allured thousands to their inevitable destruction. It is a captivating sin that leads away the sinner in triumph; they cannot deliver their souls; *Prov.* 7:22: 'He goeth after her straightway, as an ox goeth to the slaughter, or as a fool to the correction of the stocks.' Mark, a fool; it maddens and befools men, takes away their understanding; the Septuagint renders it, 'as a dog by the collar'; or as we might say, a dog on a string.

I have read of one that, having by this sin wasted his body, was told by physicians, that except he left it, he would quickly lose his eyes: he answered, if it be so, then *vale lumen amicum*, farewell sweet light. And I remember that Luther writes of a certain nobleman in his country, who was so besotted with the sin of whoredom that he was not ashamed to say that if he might live here for ever, and be carried from one brothel to another, he would never desire any other heaven. The greatest conquerors that have subdued kingdoms and scorned to be commanded by any have been miserably enslaved and captivated by this lust.

Oh, think sadly upon this argument! God often gives them up to impenitency, and will not spend a rod upon them to reclaim them. See *Hos.* 4:14; *Rev.* 22:11.

Argument 7

Those few that have been recovered by repentance out of it, Oh how bitter has God made it to their souls!

'I find it (says Solomon) more bitter than death', *Eccles.* 7:26. Death is a very bitter thing; Oh, what a struggling and reluctance is there in nature against it; but this is more bitter. Poor David found it so, when he roared under those bloody lashes of conscience for it, in *Psa.* 51.

Ah! when the Lord shall open the poor sinner's eyes, to see the horror and guilt he has hereby contracted upon his own poor soul, it will haunt him as a ghost, day and night, and terrify his soul with dreadful forms and representations!

Oh, dear-bought pleasure, if this were all it should cost! What is now become of the pleasure of sin? Oh what gall and wormwood will you taste, when once the Lord shall bring you to a sight of it! The Hebrew word for repentance (*Nacham*) signifies *an irking of the soul,* and the Greek word (*Metamelia*), signifies *after-grief:* Yea, it is called, a rending of the heart, as if it were torn in pieces in a man's breast. Ask such a poor soul what it thinks of such courses now! Oh! now it loathes, abhors itself for them.

Ask him, if he dares sin in that kind again? 'You may as well ask me' (will he answer) 'whether I will thrust my hand into the fire.' Oh! it breeds an indignation in him against himself. That word (indignation) in 2 *Cor.* 7:11 signifies the rising of the stomach with very rage, and being sick with anger.

Religious wrath is the fiercest wrath. Oh what a furnace is the breast of a poor penitent! What fumes, what heats do abound in it, whilst the sin is even before him, and the sense of the guilt upon him? One night of carnal pleasure will keep you many days and nights upon the rack of horror, if ever God give you repentance unto life.

Argument 8

And if you never repent, as indeed but few do that fall into this sin, then consider how God will follow you with eternal vengeance: you shall have flaming fire for burning lust.

This is a sin that has the scent of fire and brimstone with it, wherever you meet with it in Scripture. The harlot's guests are lodged in the depths of hell, *Prov.* 9:18. No more perfumed beds; they must now lie down in flames.

Whoremongers shall have their part in the lake that burns with fire and brimstone; which is the second death, *Rev.* 21:8.

Such shall not inherit the kingdom of God and Christ, 1 *Cor.* 6:9. No dog shall come into the New Jerusalem; there shall in no wise enter in any thing that defiles, or that works abomination.

You have spent your strength upon sin, and now God sets himself a work to show the glory of his power in punishing, *Rom.* 9:22. The wrath of God is transacted upon them in hell by his own immediate hand, *Heb.* 10:30.

Because no creature is strong enough to convey all his wrath, and it must all be poured out upon them, therefore he himself will torment them for ever with his own immediate power: now he will stir up all his wrath, and sinners shall know the price of their pleasures.

The punishment of Sodom is a little map of hell, as I may say. Oh how terrible a day was that upon those unclean wretches!

But that fire was not of many days continuance: when it had consumed them, and their houses, it went out for want of matter: but here, the breath of the Lord, like a stream of brimstone, kindles it. The pleasure was quickly gone, but the sting and torment abide for ever. 'Who knoweth the power of his anger? Even according to his fear, so is his wrath', *Psa.* 90:11.

Oh consider, how will his almighty power rack and torment you! Think on this when sin comes with a smiling face towards you in the temptation. Oh think! If the human nature of Christ recoiled, when his cup of wrath was given him to drink; if he were sore amazed at it, how shall you, a poor worm, bear and grapple with it for ever?

ARGUMENT 9

Consider further, how closely soever you carry your wickedness in this world, though it should never be discovered here, yet there is a day coming when all will out, and that before angels and men.

God will rip up your secret sins in the face of that great congregation at the day of judgment: then that which was done in secret shall be proclaimed as upon the house-top, *Luke* 12:3. 'Then God will judge the secrets of men', *Rom.* 2:16, 'The hidden things of darkness will be brought into the open light.'

Sinner, there will be no skulking for you in the grave, no declining this bar; you refused, indeed, to come to the *throne of grace,* when God invited you, but there will be no refusing to appear before the *bar of justice,* when Christ shall summon you.

And as you cannot decline appearing, so neither can you then palliate and hide your wickedness any longer; for then shall the books be opened; the book of God's omniscience, and the book of your own conscience, wherein all your secret villany is recorded: for though it ceased to speak to you, yet it ceased not to write and record your actions.

If your shameful sins should be divulged now, it would make you tear off your hair with indignation; but then all will be discovered: angels and men shall point at you, and say, Lo, this is the man, this is he that carried it so smoothly in the world.

Mr Thomas Fuller relates a story of Ottokar, king of Bohemia, 'who refusing to do his homage to Rudolphus, the first emperor, being at last sorely chastised, with war, condescended to do him homage privately in a tent; but, the tent was so contrived by the emperor's servants (says the historian) that, by drawing one cord, it was taken all away, and so Ottokar was presented on his knees, doing homage to the emperor in the view of three armies.'

O sirs, you think to carry it closely, you wait for the twilight, that none may see you; but, alas! it will be to no end, this day will discover it; and then what confusion and everlasting shame will cover you! Will not this work, then?

ARGUMENT 10

Lastly, consider but one thing more, and I have done. By this sin you do not only damn your own soul, but draw another to hell with you.

This sin is not as a single bullet that kills but one, but as a chain-shot, it kills many, two at least, unless God give repentance. And if he should give you repentance, yet the other party may never repent, and so perish for ever through your wickedness; and oh! what a sad consideration will that be to you, that such a poor soul is in hell, or likely to go there by your means!

You have made fast a snare upon a soul, which you cannot untie; you have done that which may be a matter of sorrow to you as long as you live; but though you can grieve for it, you cannot remedy it.

In other sins it is not so: if you had stolen another's goods, restitution might be made to the injured party, but here can be none: if you had murdered another, your sin was your own, not his that was murdered by you: but this is a complicated sin, defiling both at once; and if neither repent, then, oh! what a sad greeting will these poor wretches have in hell! how will they curse the day that ever they saw each other's face! O what an aggravation of their misery will this be!

For look, as it will be matter of joy in heaven, to behold such there as we have been instrumental to save, so must it needs be a stinging aggravation of the misery of the damned to look upon those who have been the instruments and means of their damnation.

Oh, I think if there be any tenderness at all in your conscience, if this sin has not totally brawned and stupefied you, these arguments should pierce like a sword through your guilty soul.

Reader, I beseech you, by the mercies of God, if you have defiled your soul by this abominable sin, speedily to repent, Oh, get the blood of sprinkling upon you; there is yet mercy for such a wretch as you are, if you will accept the terms of it. 'Such were some of you, but ye are washed', 1 *Cor.* 6:11. Publicans and harlots may enter into the kingdom of God, *Matt.* 21:51.

Though but few such are recovered, yet how do you know but the hand of mercy may pull you as a brand out of the fire, if now you will return and seek it with tears? Though it be a *fire that consumesth unto destruction*, as Job calls it, *Job* 31:12, yet it is not an unquenchable fire, the blood of Christ can quench it.

And for you whom God has kept hitherto from the contagion of it, Oh, bless the Lord, and use all God's means for the prevention of it. The seeds of this sin are in your nature; no thanks to you, but to restraining grace, that you are not delivered up to it also.

And that you may be kept out of this pit, conscientiously practise these few directions.

DIRECTION 1

Beg of God a clean heart, renewed and sanctified by saving grace.

All other endeavours do but palliate a cure: the root of this is deep in thy nature; Oh, get that mortified, *Matt.* 15:19, 'Out of the heart proceed fornication, adulteries.' 1 *Pet.* 2:11, 'Abstain from fleshly lusts . . . having your conversation honest.'

The lust must first be subdued, before the conversation can be honest.

DIRECTION 2

*Walk in the fear of God all the day long,
and in the sense of his omniscient eye
that is ever upon thee.*

This kept Joseph from this sin, *Gen.*
39:9. 'How can I do this wickedness and
sin against God?' Consider, 'The darkness hidest not from him, but shineth as
the light.' If you could find a place where
the eye of God should not discover you,
it were somewhat; you dare not to act this
wickedness in the presence of a child, and
will you adventure to commit it before
the face of God? See that argument, *Prov.*
5:20–21, 'And why wilt thou, my son, be

ravished with a strange woman, and embrace the bosom of a stranger? For the ways of man are before the eyes of the LORD, and he pondereth all his goings.'

DIRECTION 3

Avoid lewd company, and the society of unclean persons; they are but panderers for lust. Evil communication corrupts good manners.

The tongues of sinners do cast fire-balls into the hearts of each other, which the corruption within is easily kindled and inflamed by.

DIRECTION 4

*Exercise yourself in your calling diligently;
it will be an excellent means of
preventing this sin.*

It is a good observation that one has
that Israel was safer in the brick-kilns in
Egypt than in the plains of Moab.

'And it came to pass in the eventide,
that David arose from off his bed, and
walked on the roof of the king's house'
(2 *Sam.* 11:2), and this was the occasion of
his fall. See 1 *Tim.* 5:11, 13.

DIRECTION 5

Put a restraint upon your appetite:
feed not to excess.

Fulness of bread and idleness were the sins of Sodom that occasioned such an exuberancy of lust. 'They are like fed horses, every one neighing after his neighbour's wife. When I had fed them to the full, then they committed adultery, and asembled themselves by troops in the harlots' houses', *Jer.* 5:7–8. This is a sad requital of the bounty of God, in giving us the enjoyment of the creatures, to make them fuel to lust, and instruments of sin.

DIRECTION 6

Make choice of a meet yoke-fellow, and delight in her you have chosen.

This is a lawful remedy; see 1 *Cor.* 7:9. God ordained it, *Gen.* 2:21. But herein appears the corruption of nature, that men delight to tread by-paths, and forsake the way which God has appointed. As that divine poet, Mr George Herbert, says,

If God had laid all common, certainly
Man would have been th' encloser: but since now
God hath impal'd us, on the contrary
Man breaks the fence, and every ground will plough.
O what were man, might he himself misplace!
Sure to be cross he would shift feet and face.

Stolen waters are sweeter to them than those waters they might lawfully drink at their own fountain: but withal know, it is not the having, but the delighting in a lawful wife, as God requires you to do, that must be a fence against this sin. So Solomon, *Prov.* 5:19: 'Let her be as the loving hind, and pleasant roe; let her breasts satisfy thee at all times, and be thou ravished always with her love.'

Direction 7

Take heed of running on in a course of sin, especially superstition and idolatry: in which cases, and as a punishment of which evils God often gives up men to these vile affections.

Rom. 1:25, 26. 'Who changed the truth of God into a lie, and worshipped and served the creature more than the Creator, who is blessed for ever. Amen. For this cause God gave them up unto vile affections', etc.

As for them that defile their souls by idolatrous practices, God suffers, as a just recompense, their bodies also to be defiled with uncleanness, that so their ruin may be hastened. Let the admirers of traditions beware of such a judicial tradition as this is. Woe to him that is thus delivered by the hand of an angry God!

No punishment in the world is like this, when God punishes sin with sin; when he shall suffer those common notices of conscience to be quenched, and all restraints to be moved out of the way of sin, it will not be long ere that sinner come to his own place.

JOHN FLAVEL

A BRIEF INTRODUCTION TO
THE MAN AND HIS WRITINGS[1]

An old writer on the Puritans tells us how Robert Atkins, in one of his last sermons at St John's, Exeter, before the Great Ejection of 1662, took the opportunity of declaring in the presence of Bishop Gauden and other dignitaries that 'those ministers who beget converts to Christ may most properly be called Fathers in God'. Judged by this Pauline standard, Atkins' Devonshire

[1] From *The Banner of Truth* magazine, September 1968.

colleague, John Flavel, belonged to the front rank of 'Fathers'. So, at any rate, thought his first biographer who says, 'God crowned his labours with many conversions.' And so also thought his congregation who, following his death, placed a monumental inscription in his old church bearing a testimony which in 1709 brought about its removal; at that date the vicar, far removed from the 'hissing hot' evangelist who had once occupied the same incumbency, successfully complained to local magistrates about the inscription on the grounds that it was 'worthy of a bishop'!

The eldest son of the Rev. Richard Flavel, John Flavel was born at Bromsgrove, Worcestershire, about 1628, and thus spent his childhood in the stormy years which led up to the English Civil War in 1642. Following the defeat of the Royalist cause he 'plied his studies hard' as a commoner at University College, Oxford, and then, in 1650, entered the ministry to share in that sunny decade of spiritual reaping which preceded the restoration of Charles II. Speaking of the privilege of being born in the 17th century, and contrasting the then conditions with the 'many hundred years' of paganism in England and also with 'those later miserable days, in which Queen Mary sent so many hundreds to heaven in a fiery chariot', Flavel once urged his hearers to observe the special care of Providence:

> that our turn to be brought upon the stage of this world was graciously reserved for better days . . . We are not only furnished with the best room in this great house, but, before we were put into it, it was swept with the besom

of national reformation from idolatry; yea, and washed by the blood of martyrs from popish filthiness, and adorned with gospel-lights, shining in as great lustre in our days, as ever they did since the apostles' days ... If Plato could bless God that he was born in Greece and brought up in the time of Socrates, much more cause have you to admire Providence that you were born in England and brought up in gospel days here.

Flavel's life and work was carried on in the county of Devon, first in the country parish of Deptford and from 1656 in the thriving seaport of Dartmouth. Protestantism had been established in Devon early; half a century before the Puritan preacher John Barlow of Plymouth had bidden the people to remember that as 'that matchless Peer' Sir Francis Drake had spared nothing to establish a water supply for the town, so they also had a higher duty: 'Shall we never be at any charge to cause the water of life to flow through the towns and places about us by the conduits of faithful preachers?' Certainly the gospel spread mightily amongst the seafaring homes of the South West, and to the inhabitants of Dartmouth Flavel could write in 1671:

> You are a people that were born under, and bred up with the Gospel. It has been your singular privilege, above many towns and parishes in England, to enjoy more than sixty years together an able and fruitful ministry among you ... And it must be owned to your praise that you testified more respect to the Gospel than many other places have done.

Through the last years of the Protectorate and until that August day in

1662 when about 120 ministers in Devon and approaching 1,800 in England as a whole were turned out of their livings for failing to comply with the terms of the Act of Uniformity, Flavel preached every week at Townstall, the mother-church which stood on the hill outside the town, and fortnightly at the Wednesday Lecture in Dartmouth. Thereafter he took his place in the suffering ranks of the nonconformists and had a full share of the persecution which with greater or less intensity, and short intermissions, was to continue until James II fled the country in 1688.

The repressive legislation which followed 1662, while it broke the evangelical ministry of England in a public sense, scattered gospel light into new areas and led not infrequently to the use of strange pulpits.

We hear of Flavel preaching at midnight in the great hall of a house at South Molton; on another occasion in a wood three miles from Exeter; and – the most colourful site of all (though it could not have been a comfortable one) – at Saltstone Rock, an island in the Salcombe Estuary which is submerged at high tide: 'Safe there from the hand of their persecutors', writes Lyon Turner, 'they would linger in devout assembly till the rising tide drove them to their boats.'

But wherever Flavel was forced to wander he was never far from Dartmouth. What Ephesus was to Paul, Kidderminster to Richard Baxter, and, at a later date, Dundee to Robert Murray M'Cheyne, the Devon seaport was to Flavel: 'O that there were not a prayerless family in this town!' was one of many petitions offered for Dartmouth. Taking advantage of the Indulgence given by Charles II in 1672 (for which he and 163 of his congregation wrote an address of thanks to the king) Flavel obtained licence for a Nonconformist meeting-house in the town, and, when this was withdrawn, he stayed at his post until the summer of 1682 when his person was in such danger that he took ship to London on July 10.

From the capital he wrote on August 15, 'I am hurried hither out of Devonshire by the fury of the storm that lies hard upon me, my estate is pursued as a prey by an outlawry, my liberty by a *capias*.' In London Flavel joined the congregation of his friend William Jenkyn and narrowly escaped arrest when the latter was seized in September 1684. Declining an invitation to succeed Jenkyn, Flavel again returned to Dartmouth where that same year he was burned in effigy by a mob – and, despite all hazards, maintained a ministry among his scattered flock until that November day in 1688 when the bells of Exeter, Plymouth, and no doubt of Dartmouth also, rang to welcome the coming of William of Orange – an event which led quickly to the flight of James II.

By this time Flavel's work was near its end. Speaking for his fellow-ministers he wrote,

> We have long borne the burden and heat of the day; we are veteran soldiers almost worn out.

While visiting Exeter in order to preach he died suddenly on June 26, 1691, in his 64th year.

We turn now to Flavel as an author. In his own lifetime the influence of his books was considerable, as the story of a Christian bookseller in London during that period can illustrate. A 'sparkish gentleman' entering his shop in search of some play-books was advised to purchase Flavel's work, *Keeping the Heart*. Picking up the book and glancing at its pages the customer exclaimed, 'What damnable Fanatic was he who made this book?' However, after further conversation the work was taken with a promise from the shopkeeper that the money would be returned if he still disliked it after a first reading. About a month later the same man, changed in appearance, re-entered the shop and addressing the bookseller said:

> Sir, I most heartily thank you for putting this book into my hands; I bless God

that moved you to do it, it has saved my soul; blessed be God that ever I came into your shop.

He then proceeded to buy a further hundred copies of the book!

Of the importance of Flavel's writings in the 18th century abundant evidence exists. The leaders of the Evangelical Awakening, which at last broke the spiritual torpor of that century, drew much from his works. Jonathan Edwards frequently made use of him and Whitefield ranked him with John Bunyan and Matthew Henry (*Whitefield's Journals*, p. 583). But his usefulness was pre-eminently seen among the common people. Dr Rice in giving a description of the congregation of Samuel Davies (who ministered in Virginia in the mid-18th century and is best remembered today for his hymn, 'Great God of Wonders', writes:

> Households generally were furnished
> with a few standard works of good old
> times; and were expected to study them
> carefully. The writer has scarcely ever
> visited a family, the heads or fathers of
> which belonged to Mr Davies' congreg-
> ation, in which he did not find books
> or a remnant of books, such as Watson's
> *Body of Divinity,* Boston's *Fourfold State,*
> Luther on the *Galatians,* Flavel's *Works,*
> Baxter's *Call to the Unconverted, The
> Saint's Everlasting Rest,* Alleine's *Alarm,*
> and others of similar character.

Forty years later Flavel was still being
read in Virginia. In a snatch of auto-
biography, Archibald Alexander, who was
born at Irish Creek, Virginia, in 1772, com-
ments on how Flavel's writings were used
in his spiritual awakening, and continues:

This year 1788–89 was in many respects the most important of my life . . . I began to love the truth and to seek after it . . . To John Flavel I certainly owe more than to any uninspired author.

In 1812 Alexander became the first Professor at Princeton Seminary and before his death in 1851 he had instructed some 1,837 future ministers and missionaries in the truths which he had first learned to love from the works of the old Devon Puritan.

It seems that almost any listing of the evangelical authors most popular in the 18th and 19th centuries is sure to contain Flavel's name. One interesting occurrence is in the writings of Rowland Hill, educated at Eton, refused ordination by six different bishops, and for many years an evangelist in the Whitefield tradition. In his immensely popular *Village Dialogues,*

designed to impart evangelical ideas
through the speeches of representative char-
acters (somewhat after the style of Bunyan)
two men are introduced discussing the
spiritual help they had received through a
Nonconformist minister's widow who had
recently died:

Mr Worthy: I have no doubt, but your
acquaintance with the good old lady was
very profitable.

Mr Lovegood: Yes sir; and still more so,
as I got acquainted with her library: for
though she had sold some of her hus-
band's books, yet others of them she
had preserved. Among these I found
many of the writings of Owen, Flavel,
President Edwards, Gurnall's *Christian
in Complete Armour*, Archbishop Usher
on Justification, Bishop Hall's *Works*
and others. These she used to call her

Sunday company; and to these I had at all times free access: and about three years afterwards, when she found herself in dying circumstances, she gave me several of them as keepsakes . . .

No doubt Hill's sketch corresponds to what was a common enough occurrence at the time he wrote and it gives an interesting confirmation of the place given to Flavel.

Testimonies such as the above are not confined to Nonconformist writers. Edward Bickersteth, for instance, an eminent secretary of the Church Missionary Society and friend of Charles Simeon in the early 19th century lists Flavel as an author necessary to 'a Parochial Religious Library', and for the Minister's Library, under 'Collective Works of Protestant Divines', he says:

There are few writers of a more unexceptionable, experimental, affectionate, practical, popular, and edifying character than Flavel.

General popularity is by no means always a sure test of the importance of an author. But when that popularity continues over a long period of time and when a reputation is gained in ages when solid, experimental Christian literature is more esteemed than in our own, there is reason to take note. Certainly if the sustained regard of Christian readers is any guide, Flavel belongs to the very front rank of evangelical authors: according to the *Dictionary of National Biography* collected editions of his *Works* were issued in 1673, 1701, 1716, 1754, 1770 and 1797 – a list which could be extended into the nineteenth century and which, of course, passes over the many reprints on both sides of the Atlantic of some of his most popular individual works.

It is not difficult to set down some reasons why Flavel's *Works* have attained this widespread usefulness and popularity.

1. *Flavel is thoroughly and consistently evangelical.* He is always at work turning our attention to Jesus Christ and setting out those great truths of which every generation has equal need. His attainment in this respect is the more impressive when one recalls the long drawn-out sufferings of the period in which he wrote: his father, Richard Flavel, William Jenkyn, and other friends all died in prison. But such experiences never embittered him or led him to thrust the controverted church issues to the fore.[2] He had greater work on hand. It was

[2] Hardly a trace of Flavel's suffering is to be found in his writings. Just occasionally a sentence like the following from his 'Epistle to the Reader' in his *Husbandry Spiritualized* gives us a glimpse of the conditions in

characteristic of the man that on the day he was discovered and nearly captured by the authorities preaching in a wood near Exeter his subject was, 'Sirs, what must I do to be saved?' The reader of his *Works* will soon find how he delights to handle texts which are full of the gospel, for instance, John 3:16, 'The admirable love of God in giving his own Son for us' (vol. 1, p. 62), Ephesians 3:19, 'to know the love of Christ . . .' and Revelation 3:20 (sermons upon which run to 250 pp. in vol. 4 of his *Works!*) For this concentration upon the centralities

---

which he often worked: 'You have here the fruit of some of my spare hours, which were thus employed, when by a sad providence, I was thrust from the society of many dear friends, into a solitary country dwelling. I hope none will envy me these innocent delights, which I made out of my lonely walks, whereby the Lord sweetened my solitudes there.'

of the faith Flavel believed there was sound justification:

> Take an unregenerate, carnal man, let his life be reformed, and his tongue refined, and call him a zealous Conformist, or a strict Nonconformist; call him a Presbyterian, an Independent, or what you will; he is all the while but a carnal Conformist, or Non-conformist; an unregenerate Presbyterian, a carnal Independent; for the nature is still the same, though the stamp and figure his profession gives him be not the same . . . O my friends! believe it, fine names and brave words are of little value with God . . . To deceive ourselves in truths of the superstructure, is bad; and they that do so shall suffer loss, 1 Cor. 3:15. But to deceive ourselves in the foundation is a desperate deceit, and shipwrecks all our hopes and happiness at once (vol. 5, p. 527).

2. *Flavel excels in conveying instruction.* Belonging as he did to an age which believed that the gospel minister must be a teacher as well as an evangelist, he constantly aims at imparting knowledge. The principles upon which he acted as an instructor are set out in his excellent treatise *The Causes and Cure of Mental Errors*. In this work he presents the most convincing demonstration of the priority which must be given to the understanding if men are to be saved from the ruin of sin. This being so, the possession of spiritual knowledge is a paramount need: 'For the understanding being the leading faculty, as that guides, the other powers and affections of the soul follow, as horses in a team follow the forehorse.' Knowledge was originally part of the image of God in man, but now in spiritual

things 'man's life is but one continual error'. Of the danger resulting from this condition we have little awareness:

> Spiritual dangers affect us less than corporal; and intellectual evils less than moral . . . men think there is less sin and danger in the one than in the other; not considering that an apoplexy seizing the head is every way as mortal as a sword piercing the body. The apostle, in 2 Peter 2:1, calls them 'damnable heresies', or heresies of destruction. An error in the mind may be as damning and destructive to the soul as an error of immorality or profaneness in the life. This is not a matter of mere Christian liberty, but commanded duty; and at our peril be it, if we neglect it.

The preacher's great work is to aid his hearers towards this end by constantly expounding the Scriptures and that in a manner calculated to make men understand and value them. The standard Flavel set for others he constantly sought to follow himself:

> Truth lies deep, as the rich veins of gold do, Prov. 2. If we will get the treasure, we must not only 'beg', as he directs, ver. 3, but 'dig' also, ver. 4, else, as he speaks, Prov. 14:23, 'The talk of the lips tends only to poverty.' We are not to take up with that which lies uppermost, and next at hand upon the surface of the text; but to search with the most considerative mind into all parts of the written word, examining every text which has any respect to the truth we are searching for, heedfully to observe the scope, antecedents, and consequents, and to value every *apex, tittle,* and *iota;* for each of these is of Divine authority, Matt. 5:18; and

sometimes greater weight is laid upon a small word, yea upon the addition or change of a letter in a word, as appears in the names Abram and Sarai.

Certainly the six volumes of expository material which Flavel has left us show him to be one of the most instructive and informative of the Puritan writers. And it is one of his foremost merits as a teacher that he knew how to convey knowledge in a form which is at once lucid, interesting and easy to retain. He has plain words suited to the capacity of all his Devon hearers.[3]

[3] 'Prudence will choose words that are solid, rather than florid: As a merchant will choose a ship by a sound bottom, and capacious hold, rather than a gilded head and stern . . . Words are but servants to matter. An iron key, fitted to the wards of the lock, is more useful than a golden one, that will not open the door to the treasure.' (vol. 6, p. 572.)

There is a vast fund of illustrations drawn from nature and church history to hold our attention. Yet he does not overload his material with anecdotes; rather he uses them with a skill not found in some of the more racy writers of the 17th century. He has also a rich store of pithy quotations to draw upon, and these not infrequently add their own force and interest. Working as he did towards the end of the Puritan period he had a great wealth of existing literature to draw upon and in Flavel one repeatedly meets the best writers who had gone before him; the Scottish divines he knows from John Knox through to Samuel Rutherford, and the English from John Bradford and John Foxe, on through William Perkins, to the divines whom he describes as 'lately sitting at Westminster, now in glory'. If anyone wants to find out the best authors of practical divinity in the century which followed the Reformation, John Flavel's quotations will provide a fine guide.

3. *Flavel's writings reveal him as a deeply experienced Christian and therefore as one well fitted to lead us in such experimental subjects as communion with God, prayer, and the life of faith.* In the best sense of the word he is a devotional and practical writer. If he speaks to our minds it is in order to move our affections and stir us to attain a higher degree of Christian experience. Rarely does he handle a subject without making it speak to us, and the extent to which he succeeds is related to the way in which the weight of his own feelings comes through to us. What we hear him saying to younger brethren in the ministry tells us much about himself:

Keep yourselves close night and day at your studies and most fervent prayers: He will make the best divine, that studies on his knees . . . It is one thing to be learned in the truths of Christ, another to be taught by him, as the truth is in Jesus . . . As ever we expect the truths we preach should operate upon the hearts of others, we first labour to work them in upon our own hearts. Such a preacher was St Paul; he preached with tears accompanying his words, Phil. 3:18. An hot iron, though blunt, will pierce sooner than a cold one, though sharp.

If we knew more of Flavel's personal life as a Christian it would doubtless teach us more about his success as a preacher. Like most Puritans he kept a diary but this was never meant for publication and Flavel's is probably long since destroyed, excepting the fragment given in the biographical introduction in volume 1 of his *Works*.

But there is one episode which Flavel himself records in his *Treatise of the Soul of Man* (vol. 3, p. 57) and if – as seems to be the case – the person who figures in the episode was himself (disguised by the use of the third person) it tells us something about the depth of his personal experience.

The story occurs in a section in which Flavel is speaking of the foretastes of heaven and the glory to come with which many believers are favoured in this world, the believer being 'sick of love', i.e., he says, 'she was ready to faint under the unsupportable weight of Christ's manifested and sealed love, not able to bear what she felt'. He then illustrates the truth by reference to the experience of two believers, one a martyr, reported by John Foxe, the other a man 'who cried out under the overwhelming sense of the love of Christ, shed abroad into his heart in prayer, Hold, Lord, hold, your poor creature is a clay vessel, and can hold no more.' Those instances are followed by a much longer narrative relating the experience of a minister (himself?) who during a lonely journey on horseback was so overcome by 'joy unspeakable and unsupportable' that for many hours together he lost all sense of earth and time. Stopping by a spring, 'he sat down and washed, earnestly desiring, if it were the pleasure of God, that it might be his parting-place from this world. He said, death had the most amiable face in his eye, that ever he beheld, except the face of Jesus Christ, which made it so . . .'

Jonathan Edwards quotes this narrative in an abridged form in his *Thoughts Concerning the Present Revival of Religion in New England* (1742), as one proof that a glorious sense of communion with God is 'not so new' as the critics of the 18th-century revival imagined. But the whole passage is so beautiful in Flavel's original words that we have not attempted to reproduce it here, not even in abridgement. Now that Flavel is reprinted all can read it for themselves in his *Works*, vol. 3, pp. 57–58.

In the light of Flavel's personal knowledge of his Redeemer it is not surprising to note the way he captured the affections of his hearers. We can understand why when the persecuting 'Five Mile Act' first drove him out of Dartmouth, he and his congregation at Townstall church-yard 'took such a mournful farewell of one another as the place might very well have been called Bochim'.

And even today it must be a very hard-hearted person who can read Flavel dispassionately. Rather as we read him we are brought into sympathy with one of his hearers of long ago who, after being seized and fined severely for attending one of Flavel's illegal conventicles, declared:

> I take joyfully the spoiling of my goods for the sake of my dear Lord Jesus, who loved me and died for me. He is not only worthy to receive my forty pounds, but life and all I have are all too little for him.

No doubt this poor tanner, and scores of other Christians who belonged to his flock, would have endorsed the encomium upon

Flavel pronounced by the 18th-century evangelical, James Hervey, had they lived to hear it. He was, says Hervey, 'fervent and affectionate, with a masterly hand at probing the conscience and stirring the passions'.

In closing there is one more testimony to Flavel's usefulness which cannot be omitted. On February 25, 1838, Robert Murray M'Cheyne preached from 1 Samuel 3:19 a sermon entitled, 'God Let None of His Words Fall to the Ground'. In the course of his exposition he gave the following illustration of how blessing may follow the preaching of God's Word long after its spokesman has departed this life:

> The excellent John Flavel was minister of Dartmouth, in England. One day he preached from these words: 'If any man

love not the Lord Jesus Christ, let him be Anathema Maranatha.' The discourse was unusually solemn – particularly the explanation of the curse. At the conclusion, when Mr Flavel rose to pronounce the blessing, he paused, and said: 'How shall I bless this whole assembly, when every person in it who loves not the Lord Jesus is Anathema Maranatha?' The solemnity of this address deeply affected the audience. In the congregation was a lad named Luke Short, about fifteen years old, a native of Dartmouth. Shortly after, he went to sea, and sailed to America, where he passed the rest of his life. His life was lengthened far beyond the usual term. When a hundred years old, he was able to work on his farm, and his mind was not at all impaired. He had lived all this time in carelessness and sin; he was a sinner a hundred years old, and ready to die accursed. One day, as he sat in his field, he busied himself in reflecting on his past life. He thought of the days of his youth. His memory fixed on Mr Flavel's sermon, a considerable part of which he remembered. The earnestness of the minister – the truths spoken – the effect on the people – all came fresh to his mind. He felt that he had not loved the Lord Jesus; he feared the dreadful anathema; he was deeply convinced of sin – was brought to the blood of sprinkling. He lived to his one hundred and sixteenth year, giving every evidence of being born again.

On this fragment of history the only fitting comment is Flavel's own.

> Though ministers die, yet their words live; their words take hold of men when they are in the dust, *Zech.* 1:6.

We cannot doubt that the present reprint of Flavel's *Works*[4] will give yet further evidence of this same truth.

[4] When originally published in 1968, this article marked the re-publication of the six-volume set of Flavel's *Works* (ISBN-13: 978 0 85151 060 6, approximately 600 pp. per volume, clothbound), a reprint of the edition published by W. Baynes & Son in 1820. The Trust also publishes Flavel's *The Mystery of Providence* (ISBN-13: 978 0 85151 104 7, 224 pp., paperback) in the Puritan Paperbacks series.

For more details of all Banner of Truth titles, please visit our website:

www.banneroftruth.co.uk